Cactus City

Building a city on a lake was hard,
but the Aztecs made wooden **platforms**
to build their houses on.
The city had no streets.
Instead, it had **canals** and
people went about by canoe.
The Aztecs also built floating gardens on
the lake, where they grew flowers,
fruit and vegetables.
In the picture below, they are digging
the soil with wooden sticks.

They had to look out for enemies, because there were other tribes living in the Valley. Soon the Aztecs became the strongest tribe and they ruled the Valley of Mexico. They began to build a fine city on the islands and swamps of the lake, as you can see in the picture above. They saw an eagle sitting on a cactus nearby. So they called the city Tenochtitlan. This means 'Cactus City'.

Who were the Aztecs?

The Aztecs lived in the country we now call Mexico.
They were originally just a poor, wandering **tribe**.
In the picture below, they are being chased away by another tribe.
But in AD 1325, they settled in the Valley of Mexico, where there was a great lake, called Lake Texcoco.
The Aztecs lived on the islands and swamps of the great lake.

Contents

Who were the Aztecs?	4
Cactus City	6
The people of Cactus City	8
Markets and food	10
The Aztec army	12
Aztec learning	14
Aztec gods	16
Crafts and craftsmen	18
The defeat of the Aztecs	20
Things to do	22
Glossary	24
Books to read	25
Index	25

Living History

The Aztecs	The Romans
Great Explorers	The Saxons
The Greeks	The Tudors
The Normans	The Vikings

First published in 1985 by
Wayland (Publishers) Ltd·
61 Western Road, Hove,
East Sussex BN3 1JD, England

© Copyright 1985
Wayland (Publishers) Ltd

British Library Cataloguing
in Publication Data

Watson, Lucilla
　The Aztecs. – (Living history)
　1. Aztecs – Social life and customs
　I. Title　　II. Series
　972'.01　　　　F1219.76.S64

ISBN 0–85078–695–9

Phototypeset by
Kalligraphics Ltd, Redhill, Surrey
Printed in Italy by
G. Canale & C.S.p.A., Turin
Bound in the U.K. by
The Bath Press, Avon

Picture Acknowledgements:
Aldus Archives/British Museum, 15, 18, Aldus Archives/Museum Fur Volkerkunde, Vienna, 19; Werner Foreman Archives/National Museum of Anthropology, Mexico, 14; George Fryer, 23; all other pictures by Gerry Wood.

Some of the illustrations
in this book were originally used
in *Montezuma and the Aztecs*,
in Wayland's Life and Times series.

All the words in the text which
appear in **bold** are explained in the
glossary on page 24.

LIVING HISTORY
THE AZTECS

Lucilla Watson

Illustrated by Gerry Wood

Here is the city in the lake.
In the centre of the city
there were great temples,
where the Aztecs prayed to their gods.

The people of Cactus City

The most important person in Cactus City was the **emperor**. He was carried about on a **litter**. Ordinary people were not even allowed to look at the emperor. The most famous emperor was Montezuma.
Below, people are bringing gifts of food and cloth to Montezuma.

The **nobles** were the
next most important people.
They owned most of the land.
There were also priests.
Their job was to serve the Aztec gods.
Aztec merchants travelled all over
Mexico, buying and selling goods.
Slaves and **peasants** were very poor.
They worked on the floating gardens.
The slave in the picture above is being
told to work harder by a nobleman.

Markets and food

Here is a scene from an Aztec market.
There are rush mats, jars,
rolls of fine cotton cloth and
brightly-coloured feathers to buy.
The Aztecs did not have money.
They bought and sold by
swapping things.
So a decorated jar might be worth
a bowl of **maize** and a few beans.

Maize   Tomatoes   Sweet potatoes

The Aztecs were very good farmers. They grew maize, beans, tomatoes and carrots on the floating gardens around the city.
They also ate **avocadoes**, hot peppers and sweet potatoes.

The Aztec army

The Aztecs were always looking for
other tribes and lands to **conquer**.
So they had to have a good army.
All young men had to learn how to fight.
They practised fighting with
wooden swords and shields,
like the young men in the picture.

The Aztec army's bravest soldiers were the Eagle and Jaguar knights. Eagle knights wore a suit of feathers and a wooden helmet with a beak. They looked like eagles. Jaguar knights wore a jaguar's skin, like the one on the right. Ordinary soldiers wore thick cotton armour. They used wooden swords which had rows of sharp stones down their sides.

Aztec learning

The Aztecs knew all about days, weeks and years.
They used **calendars**, like we do.
They worked out their calendar by looking at the sun, the moon and the stars.
They wrote their calendar down on a big round stone, like the one below.

The Aztecs also had a
special way of writing.
They wrote by drawing pictures,
called **glyphs**.
Here is part of an Aztec book.
Ordinary people did not know how to
write or read glyphs.
Only priests and nobles
knew what glyphs meant.

Aztec gods

The Aztecs believed in many gods and goddesses.
Below, you can see the Sun God on the left, and the Rain God on the right.
The Aztecs were never sure that the sun would rise again each morning.
They were afraid it would be killed by the God of the Night.

So they **sacrificed** people to the Sun God, to help him fight off the God of the Night. Above, you can see prisoners going up to the temple of the Sun God.
They are going to be killed by the priests in the temple.

Crafts and craftsmen

Aztec **craftsmen** made all sorts of beautiful things.
They made fine jewellery and **embroidered** clothes in rich colours.
Painters decorated the temples of the city and **sculptors** made statues
to go in the temples.
This beautiful **pendant** is made of a greenish-blue stone, called turquoise.
It shows a snake with two heads.

The Aztecs liked brightly-coloured feathers, and the craftsman below is making a feathered head-dress. The small picture on the right shows a shield made of feathers. Ordinary people made pots, jars and jugs. Young girls learnt how to weave attractive coloured cloths.

The defeat of the Aztecs

The Aztecs lived in their fine city for many years, until Cactus City was discovered by Spanish soldiers.
The Spaniards' leader was a man called Cortes.
The King of Spain had sent Cortes and his army to conquer Mexico.
Cortes thought Cactus City was beautiful. Here, he is talking with Montezuma.

Cortes wanted the Aztecs' gold and silver.
He took Montezuma prisoner.
Then the Aztecs attacked
the Spanish soldiers.
Cortes and his men won the battle.
Here is a scene from the battle.
Many Aztecs died, and most of their fine
city was knocked down.

Things to do

1. Aztec picture-writing
You have seen how the Aztecs wrote.
Now try copying some of their glyphs.
Draw in as many details as you can.
Then colour them in.
Make the colours the same as in the
glyphs you have copied from this book.
Here are two more glyphs.
The one on the left means 'Cactus City'.
The one on the right is the glyph for the
emperor Montezuma.

2. An Aztec head-dress

Try to make a head-dress
like the Aztecs wore.
Cut out a band of cardboard
long enough to go round your head.
Then cut some more cardboard
in the shape of feathers.
Stick the 'feathers' round the headband.
Wait for the glue to dry.
Now paint your head-dress
like the ones in this book.

Glossary

Avocado A green, pear-shaped fruit with a large stone inside.
Calendar A list showing all the days, weeks and months in a year.
Canal A man-made river.
Conquer To win a country or a piece of land after a battle, or to defeat an enemy.
Craftsmen People who are good at doing difficult work by hand, and who make fine things.
Embroider To decorate a piece of cloth by sewing patterns on it.
Emperor The ruler of many countries.
Glyph A little piece of picture-writing.
Jaguar A kind of tiger, only found in and around Mexico.
Litter A kind of chair, on which an important person is carried around.
Maize A kind of corn.
Peasant A poor person who works on the land.
Pendant A piece of jewellery that hangs around the neck.
Platform A man-made, level surface.
Sacrifice A gift offered to a god.
Sculptor An artist who makes statues or patterns in stone, wood, clay or metal.
Slave A person who belongs to someone else.
Tribe A group of families who live together and are ruled by one chief.

Books to read

Growing up in Aztec Times by Brenda Ralph Lewis (Batsford, 1981)
Living in Aztec Times by R. J. Unstead (A & C Black, 1974)
See Inside an Aztec Town by C. Burland (Hutchinson, 1980)
The Aztecs by Judith Crosher (Macdonald, 1976)
The Maya, Aztecs and Incas Pop-up Book by Duncan Birmingham (Tarquin Publications/British Museum, 1984)

Index

Army   12, 13
Cactus City   5, 6, 7, 20, 21
Calendar   14
Canal   6, 24
Cortes   20, 21
Craftsman   18, 19, 24
Eagle knight   13
Emperor   8
Farming   11
Floating gardens   6, 9, 11
Food   11
Glyphs   15, 16, 22, 24
Gods   16, 17
Head-dress   19, 23
Jaguar knights   13
King of Spain   20, 21
Market   10
Merchants   9
Montezuma   8, 19, 20, 21
Nobles   9, 15
Peasants   9, 24
Priests   9, 15, 17
Sacrifice   17, 24
Slaves   9
Soldiers   12, 13, 22, 23
Temples   7, 17, 18
Tribes   4, 5, 24
Valley of Mexico   4, 5